AF584957

GROSS
things
animals
EAT
DR CLAIRE STEVENS
ADELE K THOMAS
HarperCollinsChildren'sBooks

Hey there, Super Scientist.

WARNING!

This book is so OUTRAGEOUS you'll never complain about soggy vegetables again. You thought broccoli was YUCK? Wait until you hear the GROSS things animals have been eating!

I'm Dr Claire, vet and lifelong animal lover, and I have discovered that every day around the world animals eat strange and repulsive things.

Dr Claire, Super Scientist and her dog, Frankie

I'm talking really wacky stuff, like **POO**, **DIRT** and even **BLOOD!**

The food chain explains how different living things eat each other to survive. Think about it! Poop is eaten by the dung beetle, the dung beetle is eaten by the frog, the frog is eaten by the snake and the snake is eaten by the eagle.

Sure, some food choices are a little unusual, but they're **GOOD** for the animals because even the most revolting eating habits are an important part of nature's food chain.

How often do you eat?

Cow
every four hours

Camel
every two months

All animals must feed on something to live and build up their energy. Some are polite and eat little bits all day long, while others are **NOT** polite and **GORGE** down their food in seconds. Some graze, others hunt, and some only eat once a year!

Emperor penguin
every three months

Humpback whale
every six months

Ball python
every six months

Great white shark
every three months

Galapagos tortoise
once a year!

Animal diets (even the **GROSS** ones) are made up of proteins, carbohydrates, fats, vitamins and minerals. Different types of animals need different kinds of food to survive, and these diets have changed and developed over millions of years.

Grossed out? Don't be! All this repulsive stuff is **SCIENCE**. It's just a bonus that it is **DISGUSTING**, **STRANGE** and **HILARIOUS**.

So, are you ready to go on a **SUPER**-scientist journey?

To be a nature enthusiast?

A commander-in-chief of curiosity?

Then prepare to be **SHOCKED**, **AMAZED** and **REVOLTED** as junior scientist Frankie and I take you on a journey through nature's **ZANIEST ANIMAL DIETS!**

EAT DIRT!

When you think of dirt, you probably think, FILTHY, MUDDY, MESSY! But not in the animal kingdom. In fact, dirt – or soil – is a popular snack among MANY animals. Strange but true!

Believe it or not, dirt is a good source of minerals like calcium, magnesium and sodium.

FUN FACT

Scientists use the word GEOPHAGIA (pronounced jee-OFF-uh-jia) to describe the behaviour of eating dirt.

Scientists use lots of fancy-pants words to describe things. These words come from Latin and Greek and may seem tricky at first. But once you learn how to break them down, they start to make sense.

In this case, 'Geo' means *earth* (or dirt) and 'phagia' means *to eat*.

FUN FACT

Minerals are elements in food that help bodies grow and function normally.

Different kinds of birds eat dirt. They do this to gain extra **NUTRIENTS** from the soil. This comes in handy when they lay eggs and raise their chicks. If you're wondering, 'nutrients' are important parts of food that the body needs to stay alive.

Dirt is also good at binding with parasites and poisons, meaning it sticks to them. This helps the bird to get rid of these nasties in their poop. Parasites are little creatures that get food from living inside another animal, and they are better **OUT** of the body than in!

I bet you're thinking, 'What a bunch of bird brains!' But birds aren't the only animals that eat dirt.

Gorillas, orangutans and chimpanzees also bite the dust! For these primates, dirt isn't just a source of nutrients. They eat it as a medicine to stop diarrhoea (super-runny poop). Strange, **YES!** But it's also very **CLEVER**, because the minerals in soil can absorb toxins that make animals feel sick. This makes eating dirt the perfect remedy for runny bums.

DIG IN

There are many other soil-eating species around the world.

In Australia, there are rainbow lorikeets, cockatoos, koalas, kangaroos, wallabies, sheep and horses.

In Europe and Asia, there are wild boars, goats and deer.

(Yep, those innocent-looking, big-eyed, sweet deer eat DIRT!)

In South America, monkeys (such as the howler monkeys, capuchin monkeys and black spider monkeys), peccaries and tapir (both relatives of the pig) eat dirt.

In Africa, antelopes, giraffes, elephants and zebras eat dirt.

PIG OUT ON POO!

That is one HUMONGOUS poop!

There are some unusual tastes in the animal kingdom, but probably the weirdest of all belong to the poo-eaters!

The list of poo-eaters is endless! Birds, rabbits, kangaroos, rats, elephants and gorillas – these guys **ALL** eat their **OWN** droppings.

Yep, there is every chance that an animal you love eats its own poop!

PLUNGING into **POO** can provide animals with extra nutrients – that's why they eat it. In fact, coprophagia is a super-common behaviour of herbivores (plant-eaters), who are always trying to get more energy out of their food.

Poop of the day!

FUN FACT

COPROPHAGIA (pronounced kuh-PROF-uh-jia) means eating poo.

You guessed it – it's another one of those fancy scientific words. 'Copro' means *poo* and 'phagia' means *to eat.* A+, Super Scientist!

The inside SCOOP on POOP

What is poo? Poo is the waste left over after the body has digested food. About 75 per cent of it is made up of water. The other 25 per cent is a mix of bacteria, fibrous matter, phosphates, mucus, dead cells and proteins. Fibrous matter is stuff that's full of fibre from plants. Phosphates are a type of acid in the body. And mucus is like the stuff that comes out of your nose.

Poo makes some people (usually kids) laugh, and other people (usually grown-ups) cringe. The truth is, poo is natural and a normal part of life. Even eating it is normal for some!

Poo can be called all kinds of things, some silly nonsense words and some scientific.

A giant steamer, CODE BROWN, doo-doo, LAND MINE, caca!

Yes, and also scientific words like scat, stools, faeces, manure and excrement.

koalas eat poo!

Baby koalas eat their mother's poo because it helps them grow!

The poop that mother koalas give their young is called *pap*. It might sound weird to us, but the pap holds special live microscopic creatures that the baby needs to change from a diet of mother's milk to eucalyptus leaves.

Pets love poo too!

Pets like guinea pigs, rabbits and **DOGS** frequently eat their own poo as well.

Guinea pigs and rabbits eat their poo because it contains a lot of delicious undigested plant matter. Snacking on it for a second time means they get even more nutrients out of their food.

Our beloved dogs also enjoy ... cat poo!

So, dirt-eaters and poo-eaters are doing it for the nutrients. But did you just ask about **GOOD BACTERIA?** Well done, Super Scientist!

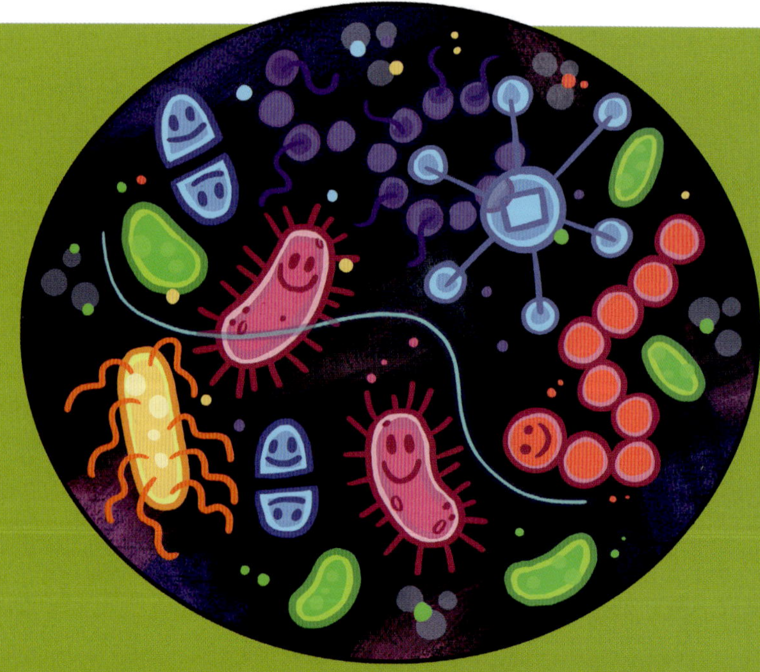

Animals eat poo to obtain important microbes. This is **GOOD** bacteria! This helps them to digest their food **AND** keeps them healthy and strong.

Eating poo = extra nutrients + good bacteria.

Bacteria, sometimes called *microbes*, are microscopic living things that are found on our skin, in our tummies and all over our houses and schools. And, of course, it's in our poo! (In case you're wondering, 'microscopic' means so tiny you can only see it with a microscope.)

DISCLAIMER: *These benefits do not apply to children! Human* **POOS** *belong in* **LOOS.**

Dung beetles – tiny creatures, huge poo-eaters!

Dung beetles don't only eat poop. They burrow, lay eggs and raise their young in it! Some even roll perfectly round balls of it before they eat it.

The poo-rollers are the most famous kind of dung beetles. These guys are super competitive and try to steal each other's dung balls.

There are **THOUSANDS** of species of dung beetles around the world, each with different behaviours and preferences. And what's more, they tend to be picky about their favourite poo.

YEP! You heard that right – they are particular about poop!

About 240 years ago, settlers introduced horses, sheep and cattle into Australia. But our Aussie dung beetles flat out refused to go near the poop! The resident dung beetles had a taste for kangaroo poo only! So, in the 1960s, exotic dung beetles were imported to do the job. And it worked! **Phew.**

WARNING! If you're grossed out by rotting things, don't turn the page!

DECOMPOSING DELIGHT

Vultures love diving headfirst into a rotten carcass (which means animal remains). These birds have **THE** most **ATROCIOUS** table manners of all animals.

FUN FACT

Ever wondered why vultures have no feathers on their head? When you're ramming your **WHOLE** head into bacteria-filled and parasite-ridden flesh, you don't want many feathers up there to keep clean! Smart, hey?

What's the deal with vultures?

Vultures are scavengers, or animals that eat dead animals. They even eat **DECOMPOSING** carcasses! *Decomposing* means *rotting*. But it gets worse! The mama vulture then regurgitates (vomits up) the rotting meat for its chicks to eat.

Scavenger animals play a vital role in ecosystems (the environments animals live in) by acting as a **CLEAN-UP CREW**. Without scavengers like vultures, there would be more diseases in our ecosystems. Thanks, Vulgar Vultures!

Beetles love gross things too

Some beetles dine on dung, and other beetles eat **ROTTING FLESH**, also known as carrion.

The carrion beetles are usually brightly coloured and flat, which allows them to easily crawl into the flesh of dead animals. They then lay their eggs on the meaty mess.

Carrion beetles have a **VERY** important job. They are nature's recyclers. We call them 'decomposers', which are animals that break down dead animals or plants into wonderful soil nutrients. This keeps the balance of nature just right!

Let's not forget hilarious hyenas!

Hyenas are famous for their laughter. But the truth is they aren't really laughing. Their calls just sound like it.

The spotted hyena is the largest and most common hyena found in Africa. These scavengers are carnivores (meat-eaters), and they eat leftovers. But don't be fooled. They are also excellent hunters and can kill their own prey.

WARNING: Did you say rubbish? No, don't go there!

GARBAGE-GUZZLERS

Eating dirt, poo and rotting flesh sounds like an awful idea. But these actions are incredibly important for animals' survival and the health of our planet.

Eating rubbish, on the other hand, is **NOT** a good idea.

Some animals, such as tiger sharks, have been known to consume **ALL KINDS** of rubbish, like aluminium cans, clothes, plastics and rope. They are adventurous eaters with very unusual tastes!

You're going to get a tummy ache!

MUNCH!

CHOMP!

CRUNCH!

These garbage-guzzlers of the sea have long, sharp teeth ideal for **CRUNCHING** turtle shells. But instead, they often use them to chomp down metal. This isn't their fault, of course.

It's just that the tiger sharks are mistaking the rubbish for food!

Unfortunately, humans around the world aren't being careful with rubbish. This means too many objects are entering the oceans and rivers and putting animals' lives at risk! **That's TERRIBLE!**

Bin chickens

Tiger sharks are not the only animals eating rubbish. In fact, I bet you've probably seen **GARBAGE**-guzzling behaviour in your own backyard or at school.

The ibis is a **SUPERIOR** scavenger and spends its days rummaging through bins searching for scraps and leftovers. Unlike the tiger sharks, these **DUMPSTER-DIVERS** are experts at avoiding plastics and metals. They mainly eat bin juice and half-eaten lunches!

Rubbish removal

Did you know that every Australian makes about 10 kilograms of rubbish each week? Much of it comes from plastic items we throw away, such as bags, containers and lolly wrappers. Once we are done with it, the plastic often ends up in nature and in our beautiful oceans. The good news is we are making some positive changes. We've swapped out most single-use plastic bags for reusable ones, replaced plastic straws with paper ones and we are learning new ways to recycle our rubbish! But I wonder, Super Scientist, can you think of ways you could make less rubbish?

WARNING: Squeamish? Don't like blood? Well... you might not want to turn the page...

BLOOD-SUCKING MONSTERS

Blood-sucking animals are everywhere. In the wild, at school and even in your own home!

Leeches, head lice, march flies and mosquitoes are the most common types of blood-sucking creatures.

FUN FACT

HAEMATOPHAGIA (hee-muh-TOF-uh-jia) describes the practice of feeding on blood. 'Haem' means BLOOD and 'phagia' means TO EAT.

Slippery, SLIMY leeches

Leeches are found all around the world and range in length from a few millimetres to 30 centimetres! That's as long as a standard ruler – ***GROSS!***

They can be aquatic (living in water) and have extra-strong suckers that attach to fish. Or they can be land-based and live in moist environments like rainforest floors. That's where they latch onto your feet when you walk past. ***OUCH!***

Most leeches have two jaws that bite into your skin. Then they inject an anticoagulant that stops your blood from clotting, while they drink several times their body weight.

GREEDY GUTS. But don't worry...the ones here in Australia are usually small enough to pull off and only leave you with a slight itch!

Terrifying vampire bats

Did you know there's a bat called the **VAMPIRE BAT**, which drinks the blood of animals? **HORRIFIC!**

These creatures of the night live in Central America and some South American countries. They find their prey by echolocation, smell and heat. Echolocation is when the bats send out a sound wave and it bounces off the object. This means they can find their prey in the dark. How amazing is that!

Depending on the species of vampire bat, they feed on the blood of birds and mammals. Large animals like cows and horses are easy victims for them. Like leeches, the bats' saliva contains an anticoagulant that stops the blood from clotting.

It's tempting to think these animals are **EVIL**, but they are not. They are simply finding a way to survive. Everybody's got to eat, right?

FUN FACT

Most bats cannot walk, but vampire bats CAN! Bat wings have long, spread-out digits (like fingers), which they use to fly. But vampire bats also use their wings like 'legs' to walk/crawl as they approach their prey.

WARNING: The next page is TOTALLY GRUESOME!

BIZARRE BONE-CHEWERS

Plants often don't have enough minerals like phosphorus and calcium for herbivores to grow normally. But bones DO have those sorts of minerals. So, bone-chewing or gnawing allows plant-eating animals to stay healthy.

This crunchy dinner menu is mostly eaten by camels, giraffes, wildebeest and antelopes in the wild.

FUN FACT

Did you know that cows chew bones? And what's even more bizarre is that they mostly chew old cow bones they find in paddocks! This behaviour is only seen in cows that have a phosphorus deficiency.

Pets love bones too

Dogs think bones are the **BEST** thing ever, and cats don't mind a nibble either.

But we have to be very careful with feeding bones to pets. They can get stuck in their throats and tummies, and cause big problems. It's important that we **NEVER** give cooked bones to our pets.

Even tortoises are known to eat bones! Tortoises are calcium-hungry beasts! They need calcium to build their hard shells. And they need it to have a strong skeleton and to produce eggs. So, chewing bones and chomping on carcasses does the trick!

Cats are wild for bones

Cats are incredible hunters. They play with their food, then **DEVOUR** the entire thing **WHOLE!** Muscles, organs, skin and even bones.

There are many types of wild cats in the world, like tigers, lions, leopards and jaguars. And they are all carnivorous.

They have great **BIG** appetites too. Lions, for example, can eat animals like zebra and wildebeest, which weigh up to 450 kilograms, bones and all!

Wait, 450 kilograms? That's more than a **GRAND PIANO!**

FUN FACT

OSTEOPHAGIA
(pronounced os-tee-oh-FAY-jia) is the scientific name for bone-eating.

'Osteo' means *bones* and 'phagia' means *to eat*! Easy, right? Okay, smartypants.

WARNING: Seriously slippery creatures ahead!

SNACKALICIOUS SKIN

What is skin anyway? It's the outer covering of humans like you and me, and animals too. It protects the body from germs and injuries, and keeps our temperature comfortable.

Different animals have different skin features. Birds have feathers attached to their skin, while fish have scales. Frankie's skin has a thick layer of fur. And some animals like snakes and the leopard gecko even shed their skin.

Leaping lizards

Leopard geckos are small (and totally awesome) lizards. As you might expect from the name, they are covered in **SPOTS**.

Leopard geckos are cold-blooded animals. This means they get hotter or colder depending on the temperature outside. And guess what? They shed their skin and...

Yep, you guessed it – then they **EAT IT!**

You see, the gecko's skin contains lots of nutrients (energy) and minerals, so eating their shed skin helps get some of those nutrients back.

Another **SUPER-SMART** reason geckos do this is that leaving shed skin lying around attracts predators (animals that have geckos on their menu!). That's never a good idea in the animal kingdom.

Slippery caecilians

Caecilians are another example of a skin-snacker. Caecilians are actually legless amphibians. As youngsters, they feed on their mother's skin. This provides the babies with the nutrients and fat they need to grow. Incredibly, the mother's skin grows back every three days.

If you're thinking these two skin-eaters are the only ones on the planet, think again...

Gutsy ground squirrel

The California ground squirrel chomps down snakeskin as a tasty snack! But as we are learning, there is usually a genius reason for this type of **RIDICULOUSNESS!**

The clever squirrel eats the shed snakeskin and then licks itself. This puts the snake's scent all over the squirrel's body. If they smell like snakes, they're less likely to be eaten by snakes!

FUN FACT

Did you know there are tiny eight-legged Demodex mites eating YOUR skin cells right now? But don't worry, they're completely harmless!

The older a person gets, the more mites they have on their body. Kids have way fewer mites than their parents. **LUCKY YOU!**

Grossed out?
WATCH OUT!
The next page is bound to have you feeling QUEASY!

CHOMPING DOWN CHUNDER

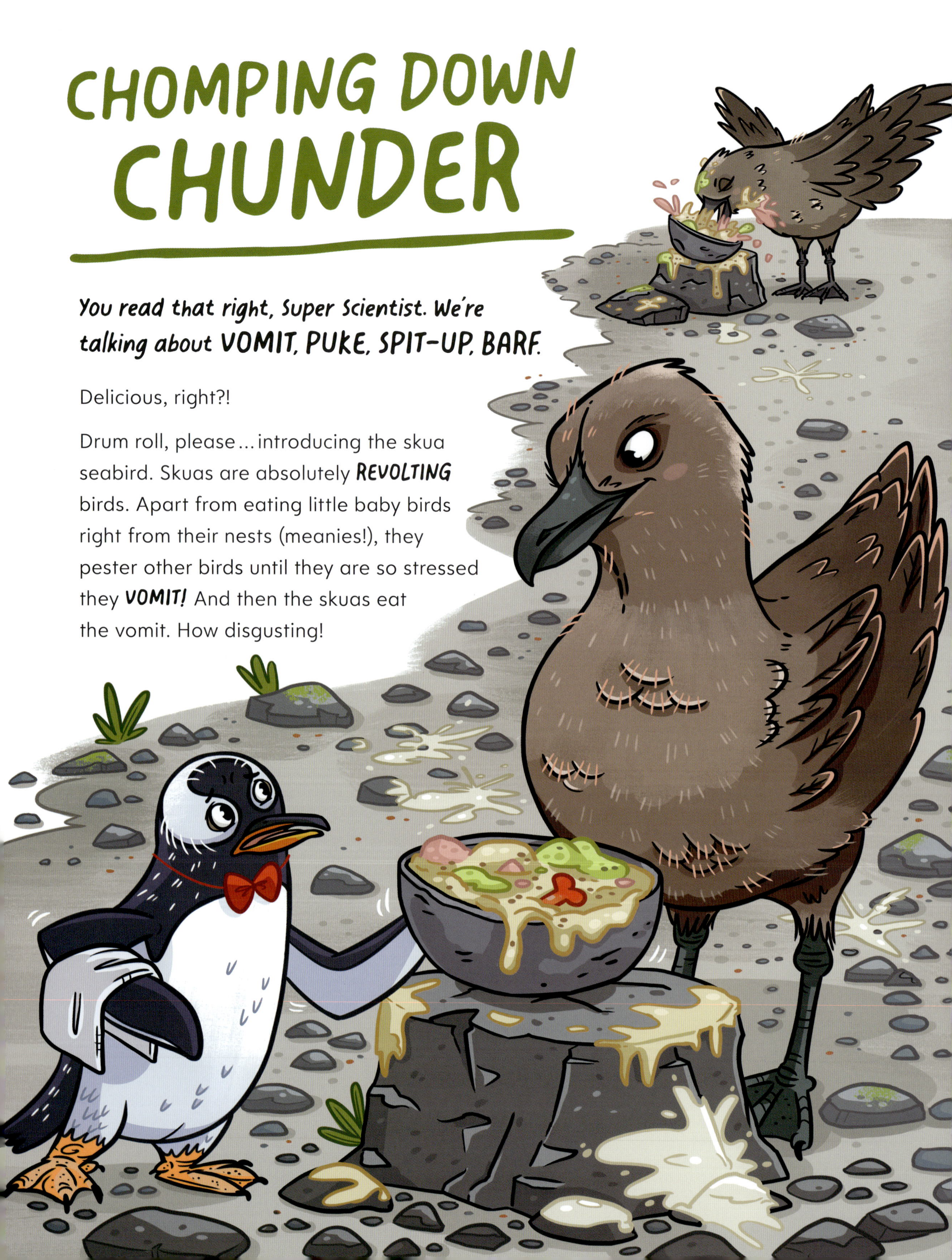

You read that right, Super Scientist. We're talking about VOMIT, PUKE, SPIT-UP, BARF.

Delicious, right?!

Drum roll, please...introducing the skua seabird. Skuas are absolutely **REVOLTING** birds. Apart from eating little baby birds right from their nests (meanies!), they pester other birds until they are so stressed they **VOMIT!** And then the skuas eat the vomit. How disgusting!

Hungry for some more bizarre barf facts?

Oh, excuse me. I've already vomited on that!

Ah, what did you say?

Houseflies vomit up special digestive juices on their food before eating it.

When we get hungry, we use our teeth to bite into food. But flies don't have teeth. Instead, they've figured out a clever way to break down their food. They regurgitate digestive juices onto their food to dissolve it. Then they slurp it up. **BLUURGHH!**

WOW! That's a whole new level of revolting.

FUN FACT

If you think a housefly's eating habits are strange, get a load of this. Houseflies taste with their FEET. Seriously! When a fly lands on a tasty meal, which could be dog poop or your sandwich, they often wander around a bit. They are NOT just going for a little walk. They are actually tasting what's on the menu.

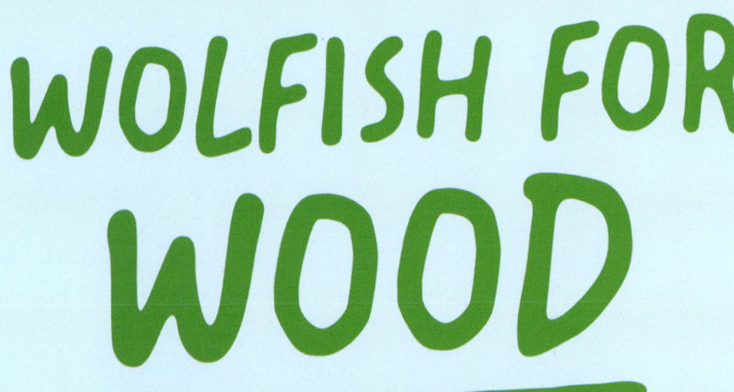

WOLFISH FOR WOOD

Yes, we're talking about wood – the thing that grows on trees…or is trees. Most of the time it has leaves, you know the one? It's that hard stuff lots of things are built out of too, like houses and furniture. It's what we use to build campfires, and we even make paper out of it.

If you were to look at wood with a microscope, you would see that it's made of tiny cells that have strong walls of fibre called *cellulose* and *lignin*. This makes a hearty meal for animals that dine on it!

Some animals eat wood because it's an important part of their diet. Others eat it because they're searching for more nutrients. Some do it because they are just plain **BORED!**

FUN FACT

There are two terms used for eating wood.

XYLOPHAGIA (zy-LOH-fuh-jia), where 'xylo' means *wood* and 'phagia' means *to eat*.

And **LIGNOPHAGIA** (lig-NOH-fuh-jia), where 'ligno' also means *wood* and 'phagia' means *to eat*.

Wood-chompers

While wood doesn't sound very appetising to us, there are plenty of creepy-crawlies that love the stuff. Beetles chomp their way through bark, leaving the trunks filled with hundreds of tiny holes. Many ants and termites love to crunch and munch wood too. Carpenter ants build tunnels and roadways through wood.

Get your big head outta here!

While carpenter ants seek out unhealthy moist wood, termites will eat ***ANY*** type of wood.

Termites love to chow down the cellulose in wood, including the wood that we build our houses with. And yep, grown-ups find this problem very ***ANNOYING!***

Different termites have different jobs in the colony. So, not all the ants go out to get a meal of wood. Some worker ants get the important job of bringing the food back to the nest for the others. How thoughtful!

There are 2000 species of termites around the world, and they live in colonies with thousands of members. Each colony has a queen, and she lays eggs. A ***LOT*** of them. We're talking 30,000 eggs a day. And this royal lady can live for up to twenty years. That means she lays over 200 million eggs in her lifetime.

After mating, the queen can be up to 100 times bigger than the other termites. She's so **MASSIVE** and full of eggs that she can barely move and never leaves the nest.

But what's the point of eating plain old wood, you ask? Isn't it rather bland?

Turns out, wood contains carbon, potassium, calcium and other minerals that animals need to survive.

Horses are known to gnaw on fences and wood rails to balance their diet. This behaviour might be helpful in getting extra minerals, but it ruins their teeth and can give them a ***NASTY*** tummy ache called *colic*.

What's that, Beaver?

The most famous wood-eating animal is the beaver!

Imagine a giant semi-aquatic (lives on both land and water) rat, with a big, flat scaly tail and two massive front teeth. Well, that's what a beaver looks like.

They might sound kind of strange, but they are **AMAZING** animals.

This super-clever rodent builds dams using branches, rocks and mud. And if there's a threat approaching, they slap their tail on the water to make a **LOUD** sound to warn their friends. **LOOK OUT!**

Beavers eat plant matter, including woody stems from trees. Beavers can chow down woodchips because of their chisel-like front teeth. These can cut through the hard outer layers of trees, letting them reach the softer, tastier parts in the centre. Beavers also have unique micro-organisms (which are microscopic bacteria) in their guts to help them digest cellulose (that's a microscopic part of wood that we mentioned earlier).

FUN FACT

You've probably heard of the famous woodpecker bird. Well, as confusing as it is, woodpeckers don't actually eat wood! They just peck at the wood to get to the delicious bugs hiding underneath.

Dogs do what?

Dogs eat wood too, often in the form of furniture. **UH-OH!** There's usually no nutritional reason for dogs to eat wood. They're just bored and looking for something to do.

But don't get any ideas, Super Scientist! Not only would you get stinging splinters in your soft gums if you tried to eat wood, but your stomach is definitely not able to digest wood. So, **DON'T EAT IT!**

What do you expect leaving us home alone all day?

WARNING: Only turn this page if you're a brainiac!

A TASTE FOR TEARS

Get a load of this! Moths and butterflies suck the tears of various animals **STRAIGHT FROM THEIR EYES!**

They drink from reptiles', birds' and mammals' **EYEBALLS!**

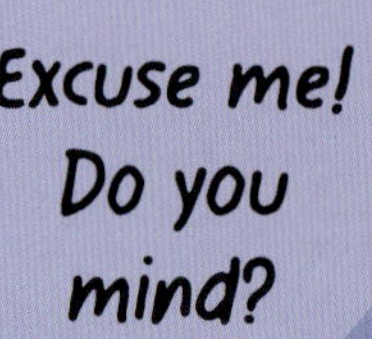

FUN FACT

The scientific term for this one is LACHRYPHAGIA (pronounced lah-CRIH-fih-jia). 'Lachry' means TEARS and 'phagia' means TO EAT.

Seems like an odd spot for a refreshing drink, right?

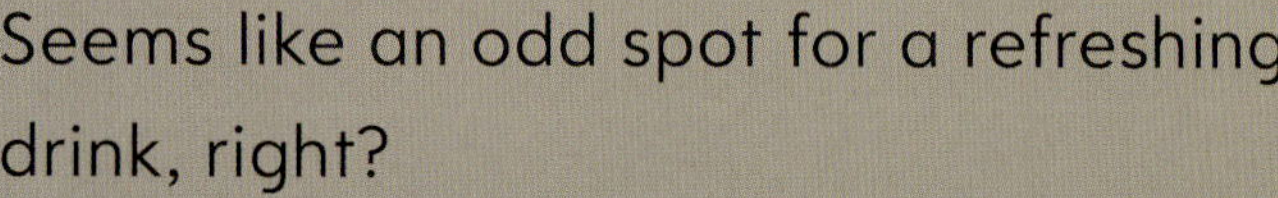

The thing is, scientists believe this behaviour is not just for hydration, but a way of obtaining salt and proteins. Kind of like a quick energy drink on the run!

Yes, another **BRILLIANT**, **ASTOUNDING** and **AWESOME** strategy to survive.

FUN FACT

It's not just the moths and butterflies displaying this quirky behaviour. It's been witnessed in flies and bees as well.

Sipping on sweat

Sweat is essential to keeping humans cool and comfortable, but some insects also need our sweat to survive.

Some insects have quite a **SWEAT** tooth.

Introducing the sweat bee! These bees **LOVE** eating the sweat of **HUMANS** for its moisture, nutrients and salts.

They are found on every continent except Antarctica (too cold!). Interestingly, these bees have tongues, and they use them to lick up our sweat!

But don't worry if one lands on you! These bees are not aggressive and rarely sting.

These guys are important pollinators for many wildflowers and crops like sunflowers, stone fruit and apples.

Think that's weird? There's another creature that secretes a fluid from their bodies in a way that will **BLOW YOUR SOCKS OFF**.

Platypuses are a special kind of mammal that lays eggs, which is called a monotreme.

They have a bill and webbed feet, just like a duck. But on land, they walk like a reptile. Strangest of all, they produce milk for their young like other mammals, but they don't have nipples! The milk oozes out of the mum's skin, it collects on her tummy and the babies lick it up!

OH NO! You're near the end!

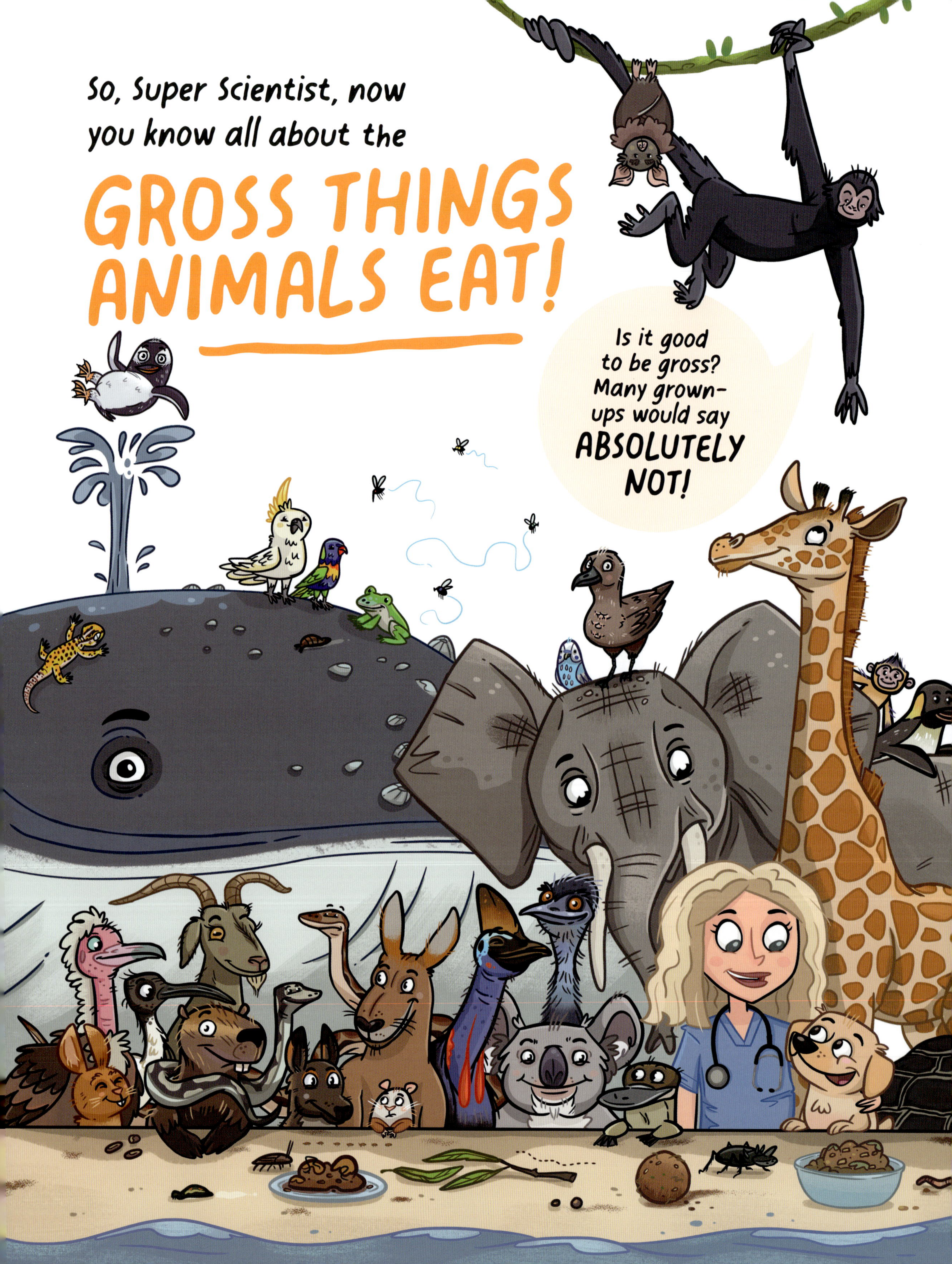
So, Super Scientist, now you know all about the
GROSS THINGS ANIMALS EAT!
Is it good to be gross? Many grown-ups would say ABSOLUTELY NOT!

But we Super Scientists know that being disgusting helps animals to survive, and that in turn keeps ecosystems (the environments animals live in) balanced. Think about it! What would happen if these animals didn't eat gross things?

If the antelope didn't eat dirt, they may not survive. If the vulture didn't clean up old, rotten carcasses, diseases would spread to other animals. If squirrels didn't eat snakeskins, then they'd be the snakes' **DINNER!**

Besides these facts being awesome, and **GROSS** and **BIZARRE**, life would be boring and unsustainable if we all ate the same thing!

So, now you know that every living thing has its place in nature. Every single animal has an important job in keeping the planet healthy and balanced.

Yep! That includes the animals that eat the most **DISGUSTING** things.

Thank you for sticking with Frankie and me through the **GORE-FEST!** Science is **NOT** for squeamish kids.

Stay curious, my Super Scientist! You're a **REMARKABLE** mastermind!

Until next time...

Dr Claire and Frankie

DR CLAIRE STEVENS

I'm Dr Claire Stevens, and I'm a vet with a love for the weird, wacky and downright disgusting creatures of our planet. When I'm not caring for pets or hanging out with my own kids and Golden Retriever, Frankie, I'm on a mission to explore the strange secrets of the animal kingdom. From blood-sucking bats to dirt-eating chimpanzees, I love sharing wild animal facts that make kids say **'EWW!'** and **'WOW!'**

I believe that even the most unpleasant animals have an important role in nature. I hope my books inspire curiosity, spark laughter and show young scientists that the animal kingdom is stranger (and more wonderful!) than they ever imagined.

ADELE K THOMAS

My name is Adele K Thomas, and I'm the illustrator of this book series! I liked drawing and colouring so much as a kid that I wanted to do it all the time when I grew up.

I really enjoy illustrating books, especially when it comes to drawing animals, gross things, food, and people and kids being silly! While I've been working on this series, I've learnt a lot about the creatures that are included in these pages!

As well as illustrating books, I work on animated TV shows and films as a designer, director, art director and producer. I have a dog called Jasper, and we live on the Gold Coast in Australia.

HarperCollins*Children'sBooks*

HarperCollins*Publishers*
Australia • Brazil • Canada • France • Germany • Holland • India
Italy • Japan • Mexico • New Zealand • Poland • Spain • Sweden
Switzerland • United Kingdom • United States of America

HarperCollins acknowledges the Traditional Custodians of the lands upon which we live and work, and pays respect to Elders past and present.

First published on Gadigal Country in Australia in 2026
by HarperCollins*Publishers* Australia Pty Limited
ABN 36 009 913 517
harpercollins.com.au

HarperCollins*Publishers*
Macken House, 39/40 Mayor Street Upper
Dublin 1, D01 C9W8, Ireland

A catalogue record for this book is available from the National Library of Australia.

ISBN 978 1 4607 6606 4 (hardback)
ISBN 978 1 4607 1974 9 (ebook)

Cover and internal design by Kristy Lund-White
Author photograph by Elisha Lindsay
Colour reproduction by Splitting Image, Wantirna, Victoria
Printed and bound in China by 1010 Printing on 128gsm Matt Art
5 4 3 2 1 26 27 28 29